Rapid Reading Series

Sue's Jewel
Book 18

Written by G. Grafi
©2021

For Rinat and Dafna:
Your twin souls whispered to
one another...mirrored one
another, and therefore, you
found each other.

A note to parents and teachers: This is the eighteenth book in the Rapid Reading series. Its purpose is to practice the diphthongs "ue" and "ew".

Follow the guide and use the tables on the next page to practice the diphthongs "ue" and "ew" prior to reading the book in order to facilitate the reading process.

Sight words are high frequency words that often repeat themselves in many beginning books. Sight words are remembered rather than read. It is recommended to practice sight words as well.

Dr. G. Grafi

"ue" and "ew" in this book.

jewel	news		Sue
few	crew		true
Lewis	stew		due
Matthew	screw		blue
Drew	blew		clues
flew	drew		Tuesday
knew	hues		cruel
new	newt		value
threw	chew		glue

Sight Words in this book.

was	family
hours	their
put	used
find	pictures
gone	saw

This is Sue. Sue got a true, blue jewel.

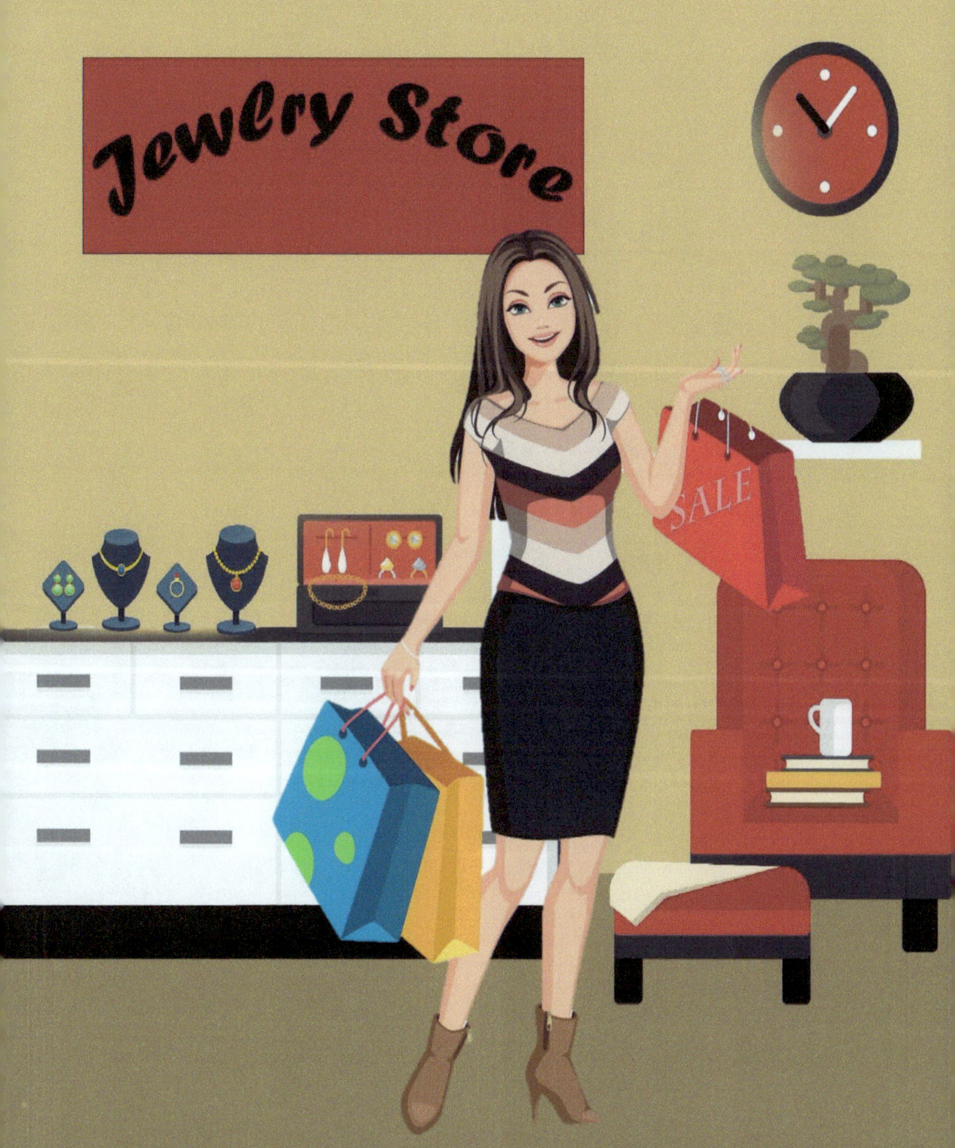

Sue was due back home in a few hours.

Sue missed her kids:
Lewis, Matthew, Drew,
and the baby.

Sue flew home
to her kids, and
they knew it.

Sue wanted to put on
her true, blue jewel.

Sue, loved her new blue jewel.

Sue threw the news and
the jewel.
Oh no!

This is Lewis. He is Sue's son.
He wants to find the clues.

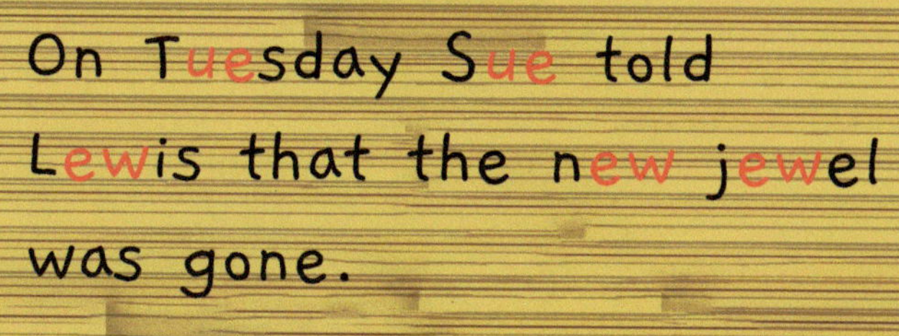

On Tuesday Sue told Lewis that the new jewel was gone.

Sue felt it was cruel that no one knew of her jewel.

Lewis wanted to look for clues
because the jewel had value.

Lewis asked the family crew
a few things about their day.

Sue made stew for the
family crew.

Dad watched how the plane flew on the news.

Lewis's sister, Drew, used glue and a screw to fix the flute and blew on it.

Lewis's brother, Matthew,
drew pictures with blue hues.

Lewis fed the pet newt
and saw him chew.

Lewis's baby brother knew where the jewel was.

But the baby could not give
them a clue until he grew.